Alan
Price

Restless
Voices

Caparison

First published in 2020
by Caparison
imprint of *The Recusant*
www.therecusant.org.uk

Restless Voices is also available as an ebook

Printed in Adobe Caslon Pro by
Printondemand-worldwide.com
9 Culley Court
Orton Southgate
Peterborough
PE2 6XD

Edited by Alan Morrison
Typeset by Caparison © 2020
Cover design © Caparison 2020

Peter Street is hereby identified as author of this
work in accordance with Section 77 of the Copyright,
Designs and Patents Act 1988

ISBN 978-1-9993746-6-2

Acknowledgements

The poem 'Purgation' has been published in the e-poetry journal *Salon of the Refused*. And the poem 'All in Good Time, Immigrant' (now revised title) has been published in a different version in the online magazine *Speculative 66*.

Contents

Poems

Wholeness is a Problem

Solutions

Restless
Voices

Wholeness is a Problem

Wholeness is a Problem consists of twenty poems that have evolved out of the letters of famous poets. Seventeen came from letter extracts: whilst three poems have as their base a complete short letter. They're called cut-ups but they could also be named cut-outs or pulled-out responses.

Taking the prose of another writer and assuming you can create a poem is technically not an easy business. You need to apply some basic, but not inflexible, rules. When starting out I was a bit purist as I wanted to use *every* word of the poet's letter including its punctuation. This left me with some workable verses but a final one that was stubbornly ungrammatical or plain nonsense (All the leftover ifs, ands, buts, ors and ins without a sensible home.) It was also a strain to use every full stop, comma, colon, bracket or dash.

A poet friend of mine told me to relax and not cut up the whole text— but only use the words that I felt suited my aim of retaining a flavour or essence of the poet's letter style—shredded in order to be viewed, through my own voice, to form a poem. Sometimes I capitalise a letter or make it lower case but the only strict rule I have adhered to is *not to add any of my own words*.

I also steered clear of being obviously random and anarchic (Dadaism is a legitimate road to take, but not for me.) I wanted another-art rather than anti-art that aimed for coherence, suggesting how the chosen poet might have attacked his or her own letter and subversively but playfully re-arranged it: whilst I, as the 'author,' manipulated their words to make them appear to be mine. It's a trick where you want the trickery to not seem obvious, hopefully allowing an authentic poem to emerge on the page.

Copyright issues make it problematic for me to publish some of the more recent letter extracts, but even only having the "out of copyright material" facing each poem would have resulted in too long a book. So I have briefly listed my sources; put them into context and placed them beneath each poem. In my notes you may then go and seek out the originals (online and /or in physical books) and discover what texts I hacked.

Here then are the fragments that make up *Wholeness is a Problem*: not forgetting of course that there are always alternative options and choices: further cut-ups to be attempted and democratically shared.

D.H. LAWRENCE

(Letter from D.H. Lawrence to Mabel Dodge Luhan, Ludwig-Wihelmstift, Baden-Baden, 10 February 1924)

Wholeness is a problem
to you, evidently.
Curb your pride,
well and good.
Make the window shine.
Polish it pure.

Give up the Karl Marx
or Lenin influence
to destroy the individual
with an introvert wash
of your cup and saucer.

More dishes
and extrovert sanity.
Humbly create balance.
No intensification, depravity
insane Americans
and partiality.

Mabel Dodge Luhan (1879-1962) was bi-sexual and a wealthy patron
of the arts who in 1917 set up a literary colony in Taos, New Mexico.
D.H. Lawrence, with his wife Frieda, came to stay and Lawrence began a
difficult relationship with Mabel. This letter is in reply to Mabel's anxious
question about extrovert and introvert states of mind. For Lawrence it's a
question of balance: always trusting intuition and instinct over the head.

T.S. ELIOT

(Letter from T.S. Eliot to Brigit Patmore, April 1919)

My love of power goes deeper than smoke.
I am always in a way the concise summary
separated from greatness.
I understand vanity as human passion.
You must attack it and recover
the stupidity of chaff
from the immense wheat.

Certainly in women's "judgement" vanity
is in part some penetrating dark result
in writing to recover
what was without profit,
that goes up, on the whole,
in disaster. There it comes,
absent of sentences.

Vanity can give you some furious word
or action that you don't appear to credit.
But it can perhaps
give half-impressed people
the first and last cut
to eventually spite me
and benefit their being.

Brigit Patmore (1882-1965) was an English writer and literary
hostess. Her friendship with Eliot, Lawrence and numerous literary
personalities resulted in her book, *My Friends when Young: the memoirs of
Brigit Patmore* (1968). Eliot's letter is in reply to Patmore's anger at his
judgemental tone. In his 'defence' Eliot tries to understand her reaction
but remains in the dark.

RAINER MARIA RILKE

(Letter from Rainer Maria Rilke to Ellen Delp, 11 Keferstrasse, Munich,
October 17th, 1915)

I, and my external landscape, drove
this Spanish angel of unsurpassable object.

The whole world displayed in Toledo
on its gazing tower, hill and bridge:

able to come together, already resolved
and experienced to begin an incredible vision.

My real task in that protected inner space
since the angel was the extreme intensity.

But how it embraces this attitude of mine
to coincide through the eyes of possessed men

and each angel-thing! Represent the inner task,
one world as it might have seen itself, Ellen.

And the utmost equivalents would perhaps
be but himself, at last, blind and gazing longer.

Ellen Delp (1890-1990) was a German stage actor and writer. Rilke's
letter is an account of his travels in Spain in the year 1912 when he was
suffering from writer's block. This drove him to extreme frustration—
especially in Toledo where he speaks of a landscape of tower, hill and
bridge (locatable in his *Duino Elegies*) requiring Rilke's symbolic angel
for a transcendental release.

LOUIS MACNIECE

(Letter of Louis MacNeice to Ms.Frances Suzman Jowell, BBC 6th
November 1959)

Stuck on either Guinness literary moods
or television champagne
too many poets,
very drunk on the radio,
are speaking of trying to write.

Owing to my own voice getting glum,
which I should say,
went two days ago
when you're this gloomy.
I'm trying to present poetry
to my colleagues
(less to be heard of please!)

Through my branch of Guinness's,
lately brewing in a rut creative awards
for behaving badly,
I have a growing party —interested employers
& the most boringly popular "in" people,
almost behaving less badly.
Lots dislike my free tape
as they are not cured
of their annual drink exams.

Frances Suzman Jowell (1939-) is a writer and art historian. In 1959
MacNiece befriended the 19 year old Frances. She was very aware of
his alcoholism. And this self-explanatory letter concerns MacNiece's
scepticism of the media and a poetry award party organised by Guiness
where boozing became the main activity.

ELIZABETH BISHOP

(Letter of Elizabeth Bishop to Robert Lowell, Samambaia May 20th
1955)

It is much more enjoyable
to have something
really finished —more coming
a lot from famous pages
than normal sex.
I discovered Yeats has 900 letters.

After lunch the tone-deaf
Olympian magnificence:
everything from him,
is apparent and felt
for all of an hour.

Now I'm eating him a lot.
Why do I feel bad —it's late
and he is just so right.
I lie down, completely calm, to imagine
being unrevealing to a kind man
until the age of 65.

Before the age of 17
I was chanting to fruit
and discovered the verse of vegetables
—you'd have a theory,
and so would I.

Robert Lowell (1917-1977.) and Elizabeth Bishop (1911-1979) were
great friends for over thirty years. Bishop's letter to Lowell concerns
reviews, learning to drive, a doll Lowell had mailed to her, the church,
her cook's baby and Bishop's reading of Yeats's letters.

CHARLES BAUDELAIRE

(Letter of Charles Baudelaire to Caroline Aupick, Saturday 4 December 1847)

I hope my perpetual isolation
has been marked,
problems warmly received.

I'm strong enough to profit
from your expression,
looks and what time remains.

The day of ones birth, mother.
So many important plans
in the name of my salvation.

Whatever terms I cherish
you will probably end in an instant,
setting aside my pride as a fault.

The course of my educations,
summarized as wrong,
has cut me aside completely.

One last time I beg you
to follow, believe and protect me.
I bring good news in my head.

The start of success, mother.
A tired wheel spinning
as I age and hurry out of life.

Baudelaire was always very close to his mother. Baudelaire's letter contains a moving passage about his loneliness, lack of recognition and the need to confide with his mother as the world is very much against him.

ARTHUR RIMBAUD

(Letter of Arthur Rimbaud to Vitalie Rimbaud, Harar, Ethiopia—10th November 1890)

Harar, Harar
I am free to remain
sedentary
in Africa
with gold,
musk, ivory,
negroes
and a camel;
and have coffee
with the willing
M. Tian:
ready when I need,
two winters away,
to return
to France,
and command
his impossible
caravan,
send on
the capital
(half the profits
are mine)
and liquidate
my business life
for honourable
peregrinations
with Monsieur Tian,
moreover
the region's products,
established
for thirty years
a good coast for this Yemen

businessman no longer
used to speaking
of marriage and for me
to continue my old relations abroad.

Rimbaud had long given up writing poetry to become a trader. His letter
to his mother informs us of Rimbaud's need to remain in Africa for his
health, matters of trade and the strong business relationship with his
colleague, Monsieur Tan. Beneath such mundane correspondence lies an
unarticulated sadness.

WILLIAM BLAKE

(Letter of William Blake to Thomas Butts, September 23rd 1800)

I met God with a plowboy dwelling in Felpham;
with arts to open the gate of my Work.

Father and the rustics are here safe
before the window at my cottage of hope.

A roller & two harrows is modest on the ground
& that is speed to the villagers of Felpham.

The first cheaper meat-morning than London
that I with the plowman give our work to you.

Voices polite & propitious go & lie with hindrance.
But I work, without accident, the happy plow

at my sweet gate. Proof the immortals have begun
to will the winds, trees and birds.

We, & not they, are meer odours. I have arrived
to find it makes greater pleasure than ever.

Thomas Butts was Blake's most important patron. William and
Catherine Blake moved into their cottage in Felpham, West Sussex in
1800. Blake's letter hopes that Felpham with its change of surroundings
will convince Butts to be even more supportive of his talent by being
more "propitious to the arts."

WILLIAM WORDSWORTH

(Letter of William Wordsworth to Lady Margaret Beaumont, Coleorton, Tuesday 21 May 1807)

A reverence for nineteen
out of twenty persons,
to make themselves images,
without a feeling of poetry,
is a genuine consideration.

People who live in a world
of striving sense
think there are neither thoughts
nor feelings but merely
pure honest ignorance.

To be incapable of Poetry,
in a broad society,
depends on human nature
to be enveloped in
my awful rank of daylight.

Poems must respect this truth
that enjoyment of Wordlings
can be absolute
among those who love life
or God Awful Wordsworth.

Lady Margaret Beaumont was married to Sir. George Beaumont.
The Beaumonts were supporters of the arts who lent out the farm on
their estate to Wordsworth. His prescriptive letter berates inadequate
writers unable to understand his work and the general lack of
appreciation of poetry by most people.

WALT WHITMAN

(Letter of Walt Whitman to Peter Doyle, 2316 Pine St. St.Louis, Missouri, Nov. 5 1879)

They call'em cow-boys
in Western Kansas

        Hundreds even thousands of them
        six feet high from hardy soil

Always on horseback
on the Santa Fe road

        Hard work to get away from
        a wild race in one principal place

I stopt in middle Colorado,
piled up prizes like in a lottery

        Some real good strikes in haycocks
        Great rough bullion at Pikes Peak

I wanted to stay all winter
at a town right in those plains

        I had some running blanks
        in the middle of Denver city

Then I had me stacks in a mining camp
— herdsmen right in the middle

        The geographies of employment
        My travel is no desert.

Whitman was on a two month tour of the Rocky Mountains and Colorado when he wrote this letter. He describes the rich and poor of the mining camps, cowboys and the livestock of The Plains in 1879. Peter Doyle, a bus conductor, is considered to be Whitman's principal lover.

PHILIP LARKIN

(Letter of Philip Larkin to Maeve Brennan, 7th August 1962)

Ah,
the times do me in well.
I should have acted differently.
All of my years
are
SUNLESS.

Looking for that adolescence
(was it everything still waiting to hardly happen?)
or
SUPPOSED
to be needed to happen...

I can't say what happens is a sign
of what may have been life's expected things,
or if those calls
are my
GOING BACK
to that

agreeable 'second prospect'
and the start of a different lifetime.

I	What
don't	I
matter	feel
for	in
I	fact
am	isn't
on	welcome.
course	To have
downhill.	most of my

40 YEARS occur as SUPPOSED
first only
strikes.

A typically pessimistic letter from Larkin on reaching the age of forty and feeling a failure. Maeve Brenan was the woman Larkin nearly married. 2003 saw the publication of her book, *The Philip Larkin I Knew*.

LORD BYRON

(Letter of Lord Byron to Lady Caroline Lamb, Date?)

My heart won't talk of you being
through something foolish
but of my greater talents.

Yet they cease to judge
now that I have you, perplexing
and absurd poor Caro.

You have more to see in general,
therefore when near you I wish
to understand, amiable beauty,

what vases, tables etc should be
thought as tropes and figures
…or nothing lives.

A being that pours a volcano
a bit colder, to make everything
dangerous.

Keep away fascinating woman
with your veins of lava!

Lady Caroline Lamb, best known for her love affair with Byron. This
undated letter is an unequivocal paean of praise.

JOHN KEATS

(Letter of John Keats to Fanny Braune, February 1820)

A black currant jelly smear,
which is excessively vile,
remains very purple.
I have licked the Quill
but the old pen is much inclined
to cause depression.

However Penmanship
which has very little mixture
in it should spring at a purple medicine.
It has made a mark on me.

I start writing disfigured thought
made up of Brown's Ben Jonson experience.
(The very best book by he of an excellent nature)

Colour pages would suit the whole week I fancy.
Still I warn you, any of those low-spirited
of style shall have ungallant blue-lines
to ascribe and impute fault
to the little I wrote well.
I am the last of the few to say it:
shaking so much of purplue nerve.

Fanny Braune (Keats's fiancée and muse.) We usually associate letters
to Fanny to be about Keats love for her or his ill health. Here is one
both sad and humouous concerning his quill and the colour of ink.

S.T. COLERIDGE

(Letter of S.T. Coleridge to 'Citizen' John Thelwall, 19th November 1796)

I cannot breathe thro my awkward nose
but my face is open with an eagerness of lips.
I am animated by the books, that I read,
to forget my expressive & monkish shape.

I am physiognomically out of the way.
Indeed my walk indicates I oppose indolence,
so my gait is all asperity in an impassioned carcase.
But I am told that my good nature is deep.

I am a sensual cormorant often mistaken
for a flat mouth, eyes, eyebrows & forehead
of personal inexpression & idiotic sloth.
(Your portrait of me measured the whole man.)

I am a great library swallowed up in eloquence.
My conversation a good immediate thing
capable of a sense of duty to overpower
the flabby energies of a puritanical opponent.

John Thelwall (1764-1834) was an orator, writer and elocutionist.
Coleridge comments on two of his own poems that have just been
published. He then digresses into a physical description of himself.

ALEXANDER BLOK

(Letter of Alexander Blok to Vsevolod Meyerhold about his play
Fairground Booth — 1917)

Any ram battering it lifeless
discloses this embrace of the farce

and the perverted forward trust
of its arms, and fathomless eyes,

begins to dull the beautiful world
to break through the old matter.

The frightful will become clear
how it strives, climbs and embraces

a young and stupid sacrificing fool
included in the wax caresses.

A response to the actor, director and producer Vsevold Meyerhold
(1874–1940) where Blok outlines the revolutionary power of theatrical
farce.

WILFRED OWEN

(Letter of Wilfred Owen to Susan Owen, 4th or 5th October 1918)

My sheer earthly faculties disturb
the perfect War talk about an other engagement!
A marching steadily back
and the sheer lost detail.
The papers are blood crimson lies.

I shot one man (I must have the censor).
My revolver. My nerves. My Abhorrence.
I fought the word-parties
that now speak to qualify these boys
whose sufferings are my own, all along the line.

I took as an officer no word —watching for a time.
Still, we entered into limits.
I write of all the order on my shoulder;
leading them (as well as I can)
to where it is not all over
with the thing.

Moreover I may yet rest well
where a head was done in by fighting.
The end curiously enough passed
by at about 30 yards!

I find lately my first order is only with them,
as a pleader with their experiences.
I help indirectly with an angel smile.

The words I didn't use from this letter to Owen's mother were the terms
"strictly private" and "In the field". Both convey the intimacy and the
public censure of the writing. The war was "nearing an end" and so
tragically the life of Wilfred Owen.

PERCY BYSSHE SHELLEY

(Letter of Percy Bysshe Shelley to Mr. and Mrs Gisborne, Leghorn, Bogni di Lucca 10th July 1818)

Ariosto, come see Mary and I,
the calm and gentle worshippers
of seriousness and showers.
We are in the good place
of true and delicate clouds.

Take the fine summer lightning
to the delicate verge of the planet.
I cannot describe a tolerant divinity,
without the impatience of thunder,
watching you and the rift in our poetry.

The great break of the mountains,
which again pleases me less than you,
ravines over the growth of sensibility.
But fading towards the pale-noon
cannot we green mountains be equal?

A brief account of Percy and Mary Shelley's travels through Italy—
descriptions of the natural environment; disappointment at reading the
poetry of Ariosto (1474-1533) and Percy's enthusiasm for translating
Plato's *Symposium*.

BERTOLT BRECHT

(Letter of Bertolt Brecht to Ruth Berla, Lake Arrowhead, 5 July 1943)

I arrived in Arrowhead to see private
pine trees and oaks in a lost playground.
Peter Lorre asked the meat king daughter
if I was living in a little fenced off forest.
It's normal to regard work, polluted by
a Chicago millionaress, as a company
bank balance story, when one can get paid
a single cubic metre of her pearls in this
artificial century of the rich.

The course of an owned actor or writer
is a high concession unless I live, as if
infallible, thundering across the lake.
Are you learning to type properly? asked
the classic speedboats girl. You do write?
We high guests discuss the job; smoking
between two sawmills. Lorre's mountain
lake continent is under my feet. I will bite
the whole menial thing.

Ruth Berlau (1906-1974) was a Danish actress, director photographer, writer
and Brecht collaborator. Brecht's letter is a savage attack on Hollywood and
capitalism. However he's also concerned about how much the movie people
will pay him for his writing!

JOHN CLARE

(Letter of John Clare to Messrs Taylor and Hessey. Date?)

Thompson turned back
of an evening
and killd a next door snake
following his wife
and the milk pails

gypseys advised Landon
to sip the cream vipers
set to cool at the door
by a mouse hole
when he was a boy

in the fens the common snake
is fond of Shakespear...
it will creep up
to hustle in poems
just above the long grass

I, Clare got worse and worse
with one viper wound
which pickd on the ancle
coming up to the boil
as I curled in the sun

This is an account of snake incidents and snake descriptions that John
Clare came across in the agricultural world of Northamptonshire.

MARINA TSVETAYEVA

(Letter of Marina Tsvetayeva to Boris Pasternak, St. —Gilles, Sunday Ist May 23 1926)

    Silly hats — a flowering of sand and sea,
            the girls pushing Mursik's carriage,
            as grandmothers
            talked to me.
            I breathed
            deeply.
            This was a real road.

Long dresses — a strange dog with square bows;
            stroking it I became engrossed
            in thoughts of a Pentecost
            childhood, plants in carts,
            the colour of sleep,
            and donkeys turning
            easily.

    The girls — children engrossed by the bliss
            of hard ground,
            enjoying some prickly bush.
            Boris, this is my real letter:
            ones committed to paper
            striking nothing
            but beauty.

A 'cry of help' to Boris Pasternak (1890–1960) Tsvetayeva's observations of children, dislike of the sea, preference for mountains and her loneliness: all revealing her spiritual nature.

Solutions

After tampering with the letters of poets, my second sequence *Solutions* doesn't actually provide answers for that de-construction but continues with other very different, even competing voices. I could have placed a question mark after *Solutions* but that wasn't appropriate as I wanted to gently shift the playful cut-up into a possible answer—a more normative poetry.

I begin with a scissors and paste attack on an NFT booklet on Georges Méliès, a hospital notice board and a letter from a surgeon. If you think that my Méliès poem is a bizarre pantomime then you only have to read the synopses of his fantasy films to see that I am only mashing or re-editing their marvellous filmic tricks into words (YouTube followers will be aware of people attempting to cut and re-score famous film clips in their own way).

Whilst my two hospital poem tamperings are a bit of mischief concerning bureaucracy and diagnosis—the patient with the little finger of his right hand in a splint is me. After these come 'straight' poems, free translations, snatches of voices of children, and a conclusion provided by two dramatic monologues that were largely amplified from my own real and imaginary experiences using an internet dating site.

I'll return to this collection's title *Restless Voices*. None of these poems ever quite sits still. Each one is impishly on the move: sprouting another voice and then still more demanding attention. It's a Babel bundle of voices: here both objects and people will have their say. From a Woolworths fruit bowl to a ventriloquist's dummy. From an uptight T.S. Eliot to a becalmed Maria Tsvetayeva. And from the purple ink favoured by John Keats to an immigrant at the door.

I've never quite imagined this small book coming to an assertive end but a kind of gradual fading out from its speaking to, and at, the reader, by voices that could undo their cuts and reconstitute themselves, beginning once more to apprehend the ear as much as the eye.

A FURTHER INDEX TO THE 1896/1907 FILMS OF GEORGES MÉLIÈS

(A Cut-Up Fiction)

The Chloroform Fiends..220 feet
Off to Bloomingdale asylum..60 feet
The Man with Wheels in his head..65 feet
Twentieth Century Surgery...130 feet
The Sacred Fountain...100 feet
The Man with the Rubber head...165 feet
Sightseeing through Whiskey..303 feet
Every Man is his own Cigar Lighter...70 feet
A trip to the Moon..845 feet
The Enchanted Sedan Chair..185 feet
Marvellous Suspension and Evolution......................................130 feet
Misfortune never Comes Alone...165 feet
The Artist's Dream..65 feet
Blue Beard..690 feet
Faust and Marguerite..65 feet
The Cake Walk Infernal...325 feet
Soap Bubbles...230 feet
Excelsior...130 feet
Coppelia, The Animated Doll..130 feet
Fun in Court..65 feet
Going to bed under difficulties..130 feet

1000 feet of film = 15 minutes

A trip to the moon on the enchanted sedan chair full of marvellous suspension and evolution. Or perhaps misfortune never comes alone. Is it just an artist's dream crying in the cave of Bluebeard? Where Faust and Marguerite fight a boxing match watched by us dancing girls doing the cakewalk infernal and are fed a fantastical meal of soap bubbles?

Excelsior! Excelsior! We laughing ladies are now as one. Coppelia the animated doll is having fun in court, then going to bed under difficulties!

These conjuring chloroform fiends knocked out the man, with wheels in his head, apparently a practioner of twentieth century surgery. He was rapidly removed to Bloomingdale Asylum. No sooner was he inside the sacred fountain when his partner, in looking, the man with the rubber head, sightseeing through whiskey, appeared.

Every man is his own cigar lighter! he friskily announced.

PRIVATELY, TRUST YOUR HOSPITAL
(A cut and paste directive)

Notice on display in Royal Free Hospital, London

TRUST HOSPITAL
Please call extension 3677 for

. facilities team leader access
. terminal cleans
. domestic shortages
. area needs cleaning
. domestic supplies
. curtain changes
. laundry
. waste, bins overflowing
. pest control
. dump the junk
. food services and hospitality
. telephone faults
. patient transfer concerns

You can request a job number
creating and maintaining
a 'Best in Class' patient environment.

(a)   dump the overflowing patient
        and domestic supplies
        terminal area
        needs cleaning bins
        please you can
        facilitates patient concerns

(b)   control telephone pest
        request a job number
        transfer laundry waste
        access domestic curtain team

(c)   trust hospital shortages
creating 'best in class' environmental junk
hospitality cleans family food
for charges and faults call a 3677

3 VARIATIONS ON FLEXIAN DEFORMITY

Thank you for referring this right-handed librarian with Dupuytrens affecting his right little finger dominant hand...he has elected to try, using a splint, at night, to try and prevent the flexian deformity from getting any worse.

(Letter from hospital surgeon to GP)

1. Thank you for using the deformity
    The sixty one year old elected dominant
    He, with librarian handed flexian
    affecting his little right Dupuytrens
    has to try using a hand
    referring splint
    from getting any worse
    at night
    and to prevent this...

2. using a splint at night
    this 61 year old little finger
    has elected Dupuytrens
    to right the right handed librarian
    he Thank you flexian deformity
    for referring dominant hand
    to prevent
    his affecting from
    getting any worse.
    Try, and try with...

3. try using a dominant librarian at night
    he, the right flexian splint
    has handed this worse deformity
    with Dupuytrens hand to his right
    little referring finger to try and prevent
    any affecting 61 year old
    from getting elected
    Thank you for...

ALL IN GOOD TIME, IMMIGRANT

It was a matter of simply opening a door.
A small action but the thought of it filled
Ivan with fear. It could tip him into a realm
of madness. Such irreparable damage might
prevent him from ever returning home,
finding his son or even explode the room
he was now searching.

Ivan had stayed calm until confronting
the presence of this huge iron threat.

BEAUTY

How perfect is
this spread-out limb,
such lazy length
of forearm, muscle,
armpit, hidden hill
of shoulder behind
the rippling stretch
of diminutive breast,
my kissing along
to provoke a smile
and firm her nipple.

This is beauty
on a bed-sheet.

A SWAN FOR MALLARME

Poet's azure sky the hanging body
written down on a chaste blank page
where cryptic signs gradually emerge.

The man has forgotten my wings!
A swan blown up from white,
slung back—ricochet and protest.

Fragment of a dice, throw of words,
symbols and casualty of the sonnet.
Unused metaphor struggling to live.

LEDA (a version of *Leda* by Ruben Dario 1867-1916)

From the shadows the swan appears like snow;
the amber of its translucent beak
as dawn passes over its wings softly gleaming
in the cautionary light.

And then on the blue waters of the lake
when dawn no longer colours, then the swan
its wings open wide and neck proudly arched,
polished silver by the sun.

This bird from Olympus rejected by love
pushes out its assured plumage, and forces Leda
into its wings raping her in the water,
a beak pecking at her closed mouth.

Beautiful, naked and crushed. She is taken.
Soon her cries turn to moans then die away
and in the overwrought foliage stands Pan
staring out envious, eyes enlarged and amazed.

THE SHELL (a version of *Caracol* by Ruben Dario 1867-1916)

On the beach I found a huge golden shell
decorated with the finest pearls.
It contained some sacred touch of Europe
as this heavenly bull crossed the sea.

I pressed its gold to my lips to sound
the echo of marine achievement.
Placed it to my ear, where it whispered
of bluish mines with buried treasure.

The saltiness that comes from bitter winds
caught in the sails of the vessel Argos
as the stars shine down on dreaming Jason.

I can hear the sound of waves and the accents
of a deep and mysterious wind...
(The shell's been formed to shape a heart.)

FATE (a version of *Lo Fatal* by Ruben Dario 1867-1916)

How fortunate the tree which barely perceives
and the hard rock that cannot feel,
because no sorrow is greater than the pain of living
or deeper than a fully conscious life.

To be and know nothing, have no definite aim
and the fear of being, terrified of the future...
and the terrible certainty of being dead tomorrow
after suffering all your life in darkness.

To go through that we cannot know, barely suspect
the flesh that tempts with handfuls of grapes
and the grave that awaits with its wreaths
and yet not to know where we are going
nor where we come from...

PURGATION

Swift railed against the need to excrete.
Detesting his breakdown. Those bowels!
Mess of fucks. Trail of piss. And the turds.
'Madam, the master's shit on a newly made bed!'

No candlelit zone of repugnant pleasures now.
The Dean's boudoir has vanished underground.
Beds of power stations beam much brighter,
recycling waste of strong anal dreams.

Waste to annoy Swiftian imitators, of modest
proposals, in the bedroom, for centuries to come.
Dig deep into the earth all nuclear Yahoos.
Long spent. Long Lived. Misty eyed for home.

DIRECTOR'S NIGHTMARE

Hated the rushes of my over-budget feature.
All wrong. It isn't my film. It isn't even film.
The producer attacks with his digital furies.

I'm running down an analogue passage.
My nerves a jangle of panic and noir.
The dreams bungled. The vision wasted.

Gunshot. Screaming. Black and white pain.
I'm all hot nitrate burning in a film can:
Celluloid organs squirming inside me.

The C.G.I. army begins its advance.
My D.O.P. footage comes pouring out.
"You'll never project it onto your screen."

I helplessly grasp at each slithering frame.
Sprockets marked by blood and good taste.
Falling —mouth agape to their corporate earth.

They kick me to see if I might still function.
Dispose of my corpse in a missable trailer.
The Deadly Director they'll never release.

WOOLWORTHS FRUIT BOWL

Mother's discarded wedding present,
peach glass bowl fashioned late thirties.
Fruit beautifully bruised. Flaked skin,
now gradations of injury,
asking for release
of her marriage
hopes.
Ripe
lemons
are absent.

THREE WOMBS

One is barren, crazy for an embryo.
One is removed. One is diseased
on the cells of the lining

One could be adapted, to grow a child.
One was extracted, no child will live here.
One is dead, child never considered.

One is fertile, carries more children.
One could be readily abandoned.
One is ready, who will live here?
One is alive, with a promised child.

Three restless voices
arguing in her head.

NURSERY KIDS

(1)

Hey, we're going swimming with suitcases
Hey, Sam and I are on the ceiling
Hey, there's a worm on the bike
Hey, I stuck my finger in a jam tart
Hey, we can put noodles up our nose
Hey, Tom spat on the book
Hey, we're American policeman
Hey, there's a fly on my knee.
Hey, there's a witch in the garden
Hey, the monster's having breakfast
Hey, we're ghosts in the dark
Hey, we've big teeth that snap
Hey Sam, you hurt me. I'm your friend!

(2)

Mother lectures on V&A manuscripts.
Father paints his Mondrian shapes.
Daughter's art is painting herself.
Wetting her tights, smearing her dirty,
unbrushed hair, babbling out words thickly
applied. Phantasmagoria of paint, saliva
and insult, rambling up the staircase.

'Rebecca darling, where are your tights?'
'I don't want them!'
Asthmatic girl ignoring
father till she hits the landing.
'And as for you!' is squeezed
loud and thick, from a tube of paint.

'A packet of crisps love, on the way home.'
She considers the treat, laughs and straggles

her shoulders against the stair-rail.
Slowly she screws the top back
on her resource
of threats.

(3)

'Right lad let's be having yer.'
'Daddy I'm eating my bloody tea!'
Charly, son of a Tory chauffeur,
wound up, tight,
further twisted by
collection.

(4)

Claudia! Claudia!
I call with Italianate cunning.
Laughing and dancing, you quickly respond.
All the Italians have left Italy.
They're inside you —waving all day.
Claudia! Claudia!
Your limbs zip back and forth.
Everything's hurled through a space
longer than your aim.
Claudia! Claudia!
Angry, I ask you to pick things up.

The masculine meaning of Claudia is limp.
How nearer to your name are my complaints.

(5)

Trip, trip, tripping the page.
Billy goats three cross the infant ravine.
On the far side of bedtime, William's hoping
they're inside a tripping good dream.
But the big bad wolf's in his day kitchen

and Bunyip and Tailypo are rearing their heads.
'Read them away' William sobs. 'Read them away'

Nightmares can't breathe by day
if buried under library books.
Now top of the pile's a tale of a giant
jam butty falling onto a dirty floor.
William fidgets —don't break the story.
Settle down for comfort,
the moral end of a sandwich.

SHE SEARCHED FOR A GHOST WRITER

Good, here is pub. Let's go in. Nothing strong for me, please. Just sparkling water. I ran all the way from Putney. Keeps me fit. My son. He is fourteen. Does his canoeing here. School team. I helped him this morning. But you know all about me being a canoeing mother. It's in my dating profile. Sorry, the drinks not right. No ice or lemon in glass. These bar people never listen. Try to sell you more things in your drink …cheers! Now let me tell you all about my dating. I do internet for two years now…met many interesting and charming men. But they don't stay long. That is the world now. Romance is so fast moving. I stopped looking for the international type… flying in…flying out. Your hopes build up, and then all gone. I met bankers…right away they make me laugh. Always joking about money. We go for a good meal at exclusive restaurants. Do you know the Torrid Landscape in Kensington? No? You should go there. But meal costs two hundred pounds minimum. The service is amazing. The waiters never cough at you. All wear old fashioned serving gloves. There is a big decorated ceiling, with shandy ear over the tables. Such bright shining shandy ear! Afterwards I was taken to the opera…Mozart. I like his music so much! I saw *Cushi fan Tut*, three times with banker, Mr.George. He explained Mozart so well—what Cushi was up to. But soon I no longer trust Mr.George. I think he had other woman. Always his mobile ringing. I think wife was checking him out.

What about yourself? How do you do on the dating? Hmmm…very much like me…a mixed bag and some of them mixed up. What, your last lady insult you? That's nothing. People need to insult you. I had one banker who roared at me, like a gorilla, for no reason. Then he apologised and bought me a silk dress. If his financial index went down, the little ape screamed and my luck went up. The trouble is men get bored so quickly. They work too hard…little time off. So you gotta keep shining for them, twenty four hours a day! Oh, you remember about me being a single parent. I met Raymond years ago. He was a managing director of insurance company. I worked there…as a secretary…then I had his baby. Today I see him little. He has young wife now. She doesn't know about me, and my son. Marry me now darling, Raymond says…I'll divorce this one…you're the only woman for me. I say no…just do your duty. Maintenance, please. But nine hundred pounds a month is not enough. I have to work. Make clothes from home. Still he pays for my son's public school. I go to gym…get fit…help my boy with canoeing. Yes… yes…of course, I get angry. But you…you are a writer…maybe you can help me? I want to write book. My autobiography. The Thai lady's struggle between Bangkok and London. I'm only forty two. But I've seen so much. Do I want get the book published?…of course …yet more important that someone turn book into a film, to make real money! My actor friend Peter Willingham had a small part in Star Wars. He played sad robot drinking cocktail, at the aliens bar. You remember that scene? Well Peter said that they only publish autobiography if you are famous, or you write up well all the sexual bits, with some spice. I already have twelve chapters. Could you help me? Do you have some spice?

I need writer ghost. Yes, someone else has read my chapters. No, not a writer. English teacher who works at my son's school. He try to edit book. I paid him fifty pounds an hour…but so slow! It's very important that I get my life written down. What? Are you the first writer I've met? No. Last year I dated Benjamin Niblo, the big American writer. Have you read his latest novel 'Purgation'…such a great book! At first I wasn't sure…too fat in photo for me. But he very insistent - sent me five texts an hour. He came to London to promote his book… such a tight schedule. TV and radio interviews. Book signing. Only managed to fit in two dinner dates. He wasn't really that fat …just bulky. But his hair different than website hair—the colour of a carrot and so curly. But I soon forgot about his orange curls. I liked the brute from Denver. He gave me great sex. And brute lapped up smart Asian lady. My best fun time was with that big writer. He could even canoe. Canoed with my son on the River Thames He was very fast…yelling…like it was the rocky rapids, back home. Yet Mr.Benjamin didn't last. All those gifts and promise! He was like a child... couldn't grow up…hold onto a proper woman. Niblo was too close to his work. Writing blockbusters and caring for all his cattle, on ranch in Denver.

God, these novelists, insurance men and bankers. All spoilt babies in the end. One night it's Thailand, then China…Korea…Japan…the super Asian highway. It's their running track for work and play and they can't stop running. Yet maybe I too can't stop. Jogging along. Getting ahead. Probably put my feet up when I'm old woman. Hope young man still want me then. Now I must go on. Tell my adventures. So can you help me? Eh? You think I need a woman's help? I should join women's writer group? No. Men are best writers. No group. Just one writer. Keep private. Don't want ideas stolen. Will you be my writer ghost? I pay ghost well. Stop! Why are you leaving? There could be favours, you know. Please stay ghost. Help me expose these men. Expose my life. I think you could do it. Hard work. But together we can try.

Stop…stay…you are slim…fit…clever. And your hair…don't worry…it won't turn orange, from the effort. I promise you!

HE WANTED TO STOP STAMMERING WITH THE RIGHT WOMAN

Ffff...for...for...give me...for being so slow. I...I...I...c c c c
can't...f f f ully relax...the ffff...first time. It's easier...ifff...if
you don't look at me...strai... strai...straight in the eye. Per...Per..
Perhaps...you wouldn't mind...looking to one s..s...s...side. Thank
you! Easier...and quicker...for me...to write things down. Tha...
tha...That was fine...I fff...fff...feel more co...co...co...co...mun... ...
mun...ni...ative on instant messenger. The com...computer...is best.
Only need to type then. That was good. We got of to a good sta...
sta...sta...start...with our e-mails. What? You would have liked a vi...
vi...vi...vi...video as well? Impossible. My stuttering would have
been to bad to watch!

*Yeah, you'd just see Frankie's ugly mug. And he looks a sight trying to get
my words out. Well, are you going to remove me from this suitcase, and
introduce me to your potential girl friend?*

Sorry, don't be frightened that's Mar...Mar...Marco ...my dummy.
Maybe I should take him out of his case. Feel more comfortable
with Marco on my lap. There, out you come. He's a little old now,
needs new eyes and ears...a bit chipped. But we've been together for
fifteen years.

*Well, she is an attractive lady. You did alright Frankie. You did alright.
If there were a dating for dummies website, then I'd have definitely gone
for you, doll. What's your name honey? Natasha? Well isn't that fine?
Russian? Sounds aristocratic to me.*

Now Marco, don't presume too much. Natasha comes from
Aldershot. That's right isn't it?

*Aldershot? In Hampshire? Home of the British Army? Not so romantic
a birthplace. But...let's call it Aldershotova, my Siberian beauty. If you
feel any chemistry with Frankie, then I have to be part of that equation.
You see Frankie and I are quite inseparable. Travelled everywhere because*

of showbiz. We're not just an act but a relationship. I know what makes Frankie tick, and Frankie knows all there is to know about Marco. So having a lady on board, and especially one as attractive as yourself, would have to be worked out....negotiated. A serious, threesome arrangement. With me in my case, when you two are in the bedroom. Tell me Natasha. Do you have a dummy of your own? A foursome would have great possibilities.

Shut up Marco…that's ou..ou…out of line. Natasha doesn't want to hear that. Do you, Natasha. Oh you do? You don't mind? What, you're in showbiz too? I thought you were an a…a…account…ant. Oh, you act in your leisure time What kind of acting? You perform with puppets!

Hey puppets are not quite dummies, but close…pretty close…sounds like my lucky day. Though I prefer a liaison without any strings attached. Hah…hah…terrible joke…but couldn't resist it. At least it put a smile on Frankie's face…actually it's a smirk. No insult intended but it's how he usually looks when talking about me. But Natasha, you're smiling. One of us guys has broken the ice. Such a big warm-hearted smile. Like you were looking after kids. Let me guess. I bet you do a Punch & Judy show. Am I correct? You do? That's great.

Is that really true Natasha? Or are you just humouring Marco? You perform at South End on Sea? Two shows live, and an online version? A…mm…mazing!! Your glass is empty. Let me get you another wine. Medium red, wasn't it?

Of course it's medium Frankie. The lady is too posh for that sweet fizzy muck. Well, Natasha, how pc is Punch and Judy these days? Domestic violence, beating dogs and policemen …quite a horror show. Frankie's act isn't like that. Though he gives me a cheeky slap afterwards if I screw up my…no…his lines.

That's not true Marco. I've never hit you at all.
You have.
I have not.
You've slapped me three times already this year.

That's a lie!
He has Natasha. So watch out. You might be next.

Marco. Marco. Stop it! I'm going to put you down on the floor.
That's better. God, Marco is so controlling. Let me get you that
drink, Natasha. You are very pretty Natasha. I can see you now
working your puppets for the children. Tell me is Judy a bit more
feminist now? Does she equally use the stick as much as Punch?

*Hey, Frankie, Natasha could improvise with that spoon, on the table, for
you. She can stir your coffee. And if you are bad. And you're often bad
these days Frankie. Then Natasha and Judy can slap your face with the
spoon...sounds like the beginning of a fine romance.*

I'm sorry Natasha. Marco, if you say another word, then I'll unscrew
your head.

*I don't care a button Frankie. Decapitate me. Why don't you plonk my
head on the table, next to the menu? Then I can sit quiet and watch you
lovely couple getting to know each other. Arrrggghhh! Arrrggghh!*

No Marco, You can just look through the window. The rest of your
body can stay under the table. There...that's done. I suppose Natasha
that your puppets don't give you any problems? Oh, they give you
other kinds of problems? Tell me, I'm fascinated. No. I don't believe
it. They get so excited after a show that they tie you up in their
strings. Your hands are so tired that you can't free yourself. You
simply wait for them to calm down and unravel.

Why don't you unravel Frankie! Un–rav–el!
Marco stop that!
Sorry...I'm getting bored.

Shut up! You know Natasha it's so rare to find someone who does
work similar to oneself. Of course accountancy is your main job, but
you don't sound like you love it. Are puppets your real life? Yes...
Yes...I thought so. Both of us are joined to blocks of wood that we
live and act through. Of course Marco isn't physically joined to me

but we have a psychological bonding…with responsibilities. Almost like being a single parent with a very young child. It can be hard to find a partner who'll take the two of us on board. I've been with Marco so long that I can't tell who adopted who. But, love him or hate him, I do need my Marco.

Ahh, Frankie thanks. You've never said that before. I didn't know you cared!

Oh Marco may be crude and in your face but he gives me confidence. He helps me forget my stammer. Of course, I can't act with Marco stammering. But for a couple of days, afterwards, I'm not tongue twisted. I once believed…naively perhaps…that my impediment could be fully cured by the love of a beautiful woman. And If that were to happen then it might be goodbye Marco.

No, Frankie. No!

Such romantic nonsense. Is that what you are thinking? Transformation. Freedom from a simple block of wood.

Who's a block of wood? Watch your language, Frankie. I ain't just an object for the trades description act.

Quiet Marco! I'm sorry. I didn't mean to hurt you. You see it's difficult to talk without him. And impossible to talk without me stammering. What stammering? What? I've haven't stuttered on a word for the past twenty minutes? You're right. God, I must have been dreaming, not to have noticed. It's you. It's you Natasha. You've made me forget things myself…my stammering. That's wonderful, Natasha. I must have fallen in love.

And why not Frankie. You see the three of us can still work together. Just because you aint screwin' up your speech, it don't mean you don't need me, our act This could change everything for the better. Make the act more detached, polished and classy. I think that would improve things… create a less neurotic routine. Yer know, Natasha, you're his new therapy. Hey Frankie, screw my head back on, man! Let me face your lovely new girlfriend...thanks, that's better. Look I'm not a bad dummy, at heart. I wouldn't harm Frankie. Make him go crazy... or anything like that. We professional dummies have had such a bad image since that old movie **Dead of Night**. Look I aint comin' to life and bumping him off. I love Frankie boy. And the way you're now looking at him, Natasha. I think you're really falling for the guy too. That's great for all of us. No more frrr...frustrating pauses. Seriously now, Natasha are any of your string puppets, single? Someone you have who'd like to be Marco's girl?

NOTES

The Collected Letters of D.H. Lawrence Volume 2 (Heinemann, 1966), pages 76/77

The Letters of T.S. Eliot Volume 1 (Harcourt Brace Jovanovich, 1988) pages 280/281

Rilke's letter is available online at https://archive.org >stream >lettersofrain

Selected Letters of Louis MacNiece (Faber and Faber, 2010)

Words in Air, Complete Correspondence between Elizabeth Bishop and Robert Lowell (Faber, 2008) pages 158/162

Selected Letters of Charles Baudelaire (University of Chicago Press, 1986)

Rimbaud's letter can be read online—https://ohkrapp.wordpress.com/2008/12/09/arthur–rimbaud-letter-to-his-mother-1890/

Blake Complete Writings (Oxford University Press, 1966) page 803

William Wordsworth. See onlinebooks.libray.upenn.edu

Walt Whitman Complete Poetry and Selected Prose and Letters (Nonesuch Press, 1971), page 1034

Selected Letters of Philip Larkin, 1940-1985 (Faber, 1992)

Byron, Selections from Poetry, Letters and Journals (Nonesuch Press, 1949)

Letters of John Keats (Oxford University Press, 1970), page 360

Coleridge letter is available online—https://archive.org > stream > cu3192410

Alexander Blok. See *The Triumph of Pierrot* by Martin Green and John Swan (Macmillan, 1986) page 89

Wilfred Owen Collected Letters edited by Harold Owen and John Bell (Oxford University Press, 1967) page 580

Percy Bysshe Shelley—the letter's online at www.wam.umd.edu > ~djb > Shelley > let

Bertolt Brecht Letters 1913–1956 (Methuen, 1990) page 360

The Oxford Authors John Clare (Oxford University Press, 1984), pages 471-474

Letters Summer 1926 Pasternak, Tsvetayeva, Rilke (Oxford University Press, 1988) pages 118-120

About the author

Alan Price lives in London. He is a poet, scriptwriter, short story writer, book reviewer, film critic for the online *Filmuforia*, and blogger at alanprice69. wordpress.com. His short story collection, *The Other Side of the Mirror*, an alternative take on vampirism, was published by Citron Press in 1999. A TV film, *A Box of Swan*, was broadcast on BBC 2 in 1990. Alan has scripted five short films. The last one, *Pack of Pain* (2010), won four international film festival awards. His debut collection of poetry *Outfoxing Hyenas* was published by Indigo Dreams in 2012. A pamphlet of prose poems, *Angels at the Edge* (Tuba Press), appeared in 2016. The poetry chapbook *Mahler's Hut* was published in 2017 by Original Plus Books. His latest poetry book is the 2018 *Wardrobe Blues for a Japanese Lady* (The High Window Press). And in 2019 a collection of flash fiction and short stories called *The Illiterate Ghost* was published by Eibonvale Press. Alan has completed a novel entitled *Dangerous Optics* and is currently working on a series of prose poems, based on films, with the working title of *The Cinephile Poems.*